Little Mitchie

HELPING NEW FRIENDS FEEL WELCOME

MAKING NEW FRIENDS

ANNE ACCARDI

CREATING YOUNG NONFICTION READERS

Little Mitchie books spark curiosity and support early nonfiction reading for students in Grades 2-3. Designed to build vocabulary, support second language learners, and prepare readers for middle-grade content, each book includes helpful tips for parents and educators to build confidence and deepen understanding of the world.

TIPS FOR READING NONFICTION WITH BEGINNING READERS

Talk about Nonfiction

Begin by explaining that nonfiction books give us information that is true. The book will be organized around a specific topic or idea, and we may learn new facts through reading.

Look at the Parts

Most nonfiction books have helpful features. Our *Little Mitchie* titles include color photographs and graphic aids, a table of contents, a glossary, and an index. Share the purpose of these features with your reader.

Color Photos and Graphic Aids

A lot of information can be found by "reading" photos, charts, maps, and other graphic aids found within nonfiction texts. Help your reader learn more about the different ways information can be displayed.

Table of Contents

Located at the front of the book, this list shows the big ideas within the text and the page numbers where they can be found.

Glossary

Located at the back of the book, the glossary defines key words and phrases that are related to the topic. These words and phrases can be found in the text in colored type.

Index

Located at the back of the book, an index is an alphabetical list of topics and the page numbers where they can be found.

With a little help and guidance about reading nonfiction, you can feel good about introducing a young reader to the world of *Little Mitchie* nonfiction books.

Little Mitchie is an imprint of:

Mitchell Lane
PUBLISHERS

2001 SW 31st Avenue
Hallandale, FL 33009
mitchelllanepub.com

First Edition, 2027.
Author: Anne Accardi
Designer: Kathy Walsh
Editor: Kim Thompson

Library of Congress Cataloging-in-Publication Data
Title: Helping New Friends Feel Welcome / by Anne Accardi

Description: Hallandale, FL :
Mitchell Lane Publishers, [2027]

Identifiers:
ISBN 979-8-89260-898-5 (library bound)
ISBN 979-8-90145-055-0 (paperback)
ISBN 979-8-90145-002-4 (eBook)

Library of Congress Control Number: 2026930164

Photo credits: Shutterstock: Cover, p1 & 3, Pixel-Shot; p 5, ShineTerra; p 7, BearFotos; p 9, Taras Grebinets; p 11, Inside Creative House; p 13, Janon Stock; p 15, Inside Creative House; p 17, Brocreative; p 19, BearFotos; p 20, Ground Picture

TABLE OF CONTENTS

Step One

KNOW WHY FEELING WELCOME IS IMPORTANT

To feel welcome is to know that people are glad to see you. They want to spend time with you. They care about you!

Feeling welcome makes you happy. It makes you feel like you belong. Wouldn't it be nice if everyone felt welcome all the time?

CHALLENGE

Who is always glad to see you? Write three things they say or do to make you feel welcome and included.

Many times, kids do not feel welcome. They may be new. They may feel **shy**. They may be different from other people.

You can make new friends by helping people feel welcome. In turn, they will welcome others. Having more friends means more fun for everyone!

"When everyone is included,
everyone wins."
—Jesse Jackson

Step Two

FACE YOUR FEARS

You may worry that kids won't welcome you. Remember that you can't decide how others behave. You only control your actions. You can choose to be **kind**.

Kindness is often **contagious**. If you are kind, others will be too.

FRIENDLY FACT

Use the "golden rule." Treat others the way you want to be treated.

Avoid groups that do not welcome new friends. **Cliques** leave others out to make themselves feel popular and cool. It is not kind—or fun—to **exclude** others.

FRIENDLY FACT

Practicing **empathy** helps you make friends. It means that you think about how others are feeling.

Step Three

TAKE ACTION!

To make someone feel welcome, start by introducing yourself. Share something about you.

Invite the person to sit with you or play with you. If they are new, offer to show them around.

CHALLENGE

Remember the last time you were in a new situation. Write three feelings you had. Write three things that made you more comfortable.

You can make a new friend feel welcome by giving them a **compliment**. Tell them you like their backpack or that they asked a good question in class.

FRIENDLY FACT

Use friendly **body language**. Make eye contact when you talk. Don't forget to smile!

Ask your new friend questions. Listen closely to their answers. This will help you find things you have in common.

Here are some questions to ask a new friend.

- *Where did you move from?*
- *Do you have brothers, sisters, or pets?*
- *What is your favorite game, food, or movie?*
- *What is your favorite school subject?*
- *What do you like to do in your free time?*

Step Four

KEEP GOING

It takes time for a new friend to feel like they belong. Don't stop being kind after just one day.

Keep getting to know them better. Keep inviting them to spend time with you.

FRIENDLY FACT

Sometimes, talking is part of listening. Try using your own words to **restate** what your friend said. That shows you listened and understood.

Practice making people feel welcome every day. Make it a habit at school, on the bus, with sports teams, in your neighborhood, and everywhere! You'll soon have many new friends.

TOP TIPS

Use empathy.

Ask questions.

Introduce yourself.

Invite them to play.

Give compliments.

Be patient.

GLOSSARY

body language (BAH-dee LANG-gwij) the thoughts and feelings your face and body communicate without using words

cliques (kliks) small groups of friends who do not easily allow others to join them

compliment (KAHM-pluh-muhnt) a comment that shows you admire or respect another person

contagious (kuhn-TAY-juhs) spreading from person to person

empathy (EM-puh-thee) putting yourself in someone else's shoes to understand their feelings

exclude (ik-SKLOOD) to leave out

kind (kinde) nice; caring; friendly

restate (ree-STATE) to repeat in different words; to summarize

shy (shye) uncomfortable around people you don't know well

FURTHER READING

Muhammad, Ibtihaj. *The Kindest Red.* Little, Brown Books for Young Readers, 2023.

Roberts, Justin. *Giant-Sized Butterflies on My First Day of School.* G.P. Putnam's Sons, 2023.

ON THE INTERNET

National Geographic Kids: How to Be an Awesome Friend
kids.nationalgeographic.com/pages/article/friend
Learn tips for making and keeping friends.

The Family Dinner Project: Conversation Starters for Kids
thefamilydinnerproject.org/wp-content/uploads/2020/03/Conversation-Starters_2020.pdf
See a list of questions you can ask new friends to get to know them better.

INDEX